973.3

THE DECLARATION OF INDEPENDENCE

Foundation for America

THE
DECLARATION
OF
INDEPENDENCE

Foundation for America

BY JON WILSON

The American colonists declared themselves independent on July 4, 1776.

THE CHILD'S WORLD

GRAPHIC DESIGN
Robert A. Honey, Seattle

PHOTO RESEARCH
James R. Rothaus, James R. Rothaus & Associates

ELECTRONIC PRE-PRESS PRODUCTION
Robert E. Bonaker, Graphic Design & Consulting Co.

Library of Congress Cataloging-in-Publication Data
Wilson, Jon
The Declaration of Independence : Foundation for America /
by Jon Wilson
p. cm.
Summary: Describes how the Declaration of Independence came
to be writen and signed and its importance in defining the
principles upon which the United States would be founded.
ISBN 1-56766-546-2 (library : reinforced : alk. paper)

1. United States. Declaration of Independence — Juvenile literature.

2. United States—Politics and government—1776-1783—Juvenile
literature.
[1. United States. Declaration of Independence. 2. United States—
Politics and government—1775-1783.] I. Title

E221.W67 1998   98-28402
973.3"3 — dc21   CIP
                                 AC

CONTENTS

THE UNHAPPY COLONIES

Major George Washington gives directions to a soldier during the French and Indian War. Washington later became a general and the first president of the United States of America.

For over 70 years, America's 13 colonies had been ruled by England. At first the **colonists** who lived in America were happy with British rule. They helped the British win the *French and Indian War* in 1763 and were proud to be part of the victory. Over the next 10 years, however, the British began to impose unfair taxes and control trade in the colonies. This angered the colonists. The French and Indian War had shown them that they were strong enough to stand on their own. The time had come to break their ties with England.

Frustrated by increasing taxes, the colonists began to protest. On December 16, 1773, colonists protested taxes on tea by dumping tea from three cargo ships into Boston Harbor. This protest became known as the *Boston Tea Party*. In 1775 in Lexington, Massachusetts, the first shots were fired between colonial soldiers, known as **patriots**, and British troops. There were many more conflicts between the patriots and British troops. On June 17, 1775, American patriots fought the British at Bunker Hill. About 1000 British and 400 patriots were killed or wounded during this battle alone.

American colonists cheer as protestors dressed as Indians throw tea from British ships into Boston Harbor.

THE WRITTEN WORD

In the 1770s there were no phones or TVs for passing information from person to person. Ideas were exchanged mostly through newspapers, books, and small, inexpensive booklets called **pamphlets**. *Thomas Paine* was a well-known writer and supporter of American *independence*. On January 10, 1776, Paine published a pamphlet called *Common Sense*. The pamphlet was an attack on British control over the colonies. It was also a cry for independence. *Common Sense* and other works by Thomas Paine inspired Americans in their struggle against England.

Because of his intense desire to free the colonists so they would be able to make decisions for themselves, Thomas Paine sacrificed everything and was eventually driven into poverty.

TO STAND ALONE

A nation that is **independent** stands on its own, free from outside control. On June 11, 1776, the **Continental Congress**, made up of leaders from all 13 American colonies, chose five people to write a statement. The statement would announce America's desire to become independent. The people chosen to write it were *Thomas Jefferson, John Adams, Benjamin Franklin, Roger Sherman*, and *Robert R. Livingston*. The document they were asked to write would become known as the Declaration of Independence. A **declaration** is a public statement or announcement of something important.

Thomas Jefferson reads a rough draft of the Declaration of Independence to Benjamin Franklin.

Although five people had been asked to write the Declaration, one of them ended up doing most of the work. Thomas Jefferson took on this difficult job because he was the best writer of the five. Adams and Franklin added their comments to Jefferson's first version, called a **draft**, and made a few minor changes. The new draft was then presented to the Continental Congress on June 28, 1776.

This painting by John Trumbull shows the signing of the Declaration of Independence.

On July 1, 1776, the Continental Congress began a final discussion over whether the colonies should declare their independence. In the final vote, 12 colonies voted for independence. The remaining colony, New York, chose to remain undecided. For the next two days, the Continental Congress went over the draft of the *Declaration of Independence*. After a few changes, the Declaration was approved on July 4, 1776, and the American colonies became the United States of America. Since that time, America has always celebrated its independence on the fourth of July.

SIGNING THE DECLARATION

The original Declaration of Independence was signed by *John Hancock* and *Charles Thompson*, the President and Secretary of the Continental Congress. Afterward this original was printed on fine paper and signed by all the members of the Congress. There were 56 signatures on this document, the boldest of them John Hancock's. When asked why his signature was so bold, Hancock said, "To be sure that the King of England knows whose signature it is."

Right:
The Declaration of Independence was signed by the forefathers so that the colonial people would be free to have control over their lives.

Left:
John Hancock was the first signer of the Declaration of Independence and served nine terms as the governor of Massachusetts.

Corbis-Bettmann

THE DOCUMENT

The Declaration of Independence was much more than an announcement of America's desire to stand alone. It also explained *why* the colonies wished to separate from British rule. It stated that a government should be based on the rights of the citizens—and that all people have certain rights no government should take away. The Declaration became the foundation for the new nation and its government.

John Dixon reads the Declaration of Independence to the people in the State House yard on July 8, 1776.

The Declaration of Independence was publicly read on July 8, 1776, at *Independence Hall* in Philadelphia. At the end of the reading, bells across Philadelphia rang with the call for freedom. The bell in Independence Hall itself became known as the Liberty Bell. On July 9, 1776, the Declaration was read in New York to *George Washington* and America's army, the **Continental Army**. Now the Continental Army would have to face the Declaration's results: war with England.

THE WAR FOR INDEPENDENCE

The Declaration announced to Americans, the British, and the world that America was ready to stand on its own. America had already fought battles for its freedom, and now it would fight many more. Many patriot and British soldiers died during the following eight years. Finally, in 1783, America won the *War of Independence*—and freedom from British rule.

Over two hundred years have passed since the Declaration of Independence was written. The original document was badly damaged in 1823, when *John Quincy Adams* tried to print copies for its 56 signers. The document has been moved and displayed all around the country. Time and careless handling have left some parts of it almost unreadable. Since 1952, the original Declaration has been displayed in the *National Archives Building*. It rests behind protective glass in a specially designed hall. It shares the hall with other great American documents, such as the *Constitution* and the *Bill of Rights*.

American colonists and British soldiers exchange fire at the Battle of Lexington, the first battle fought for independence.

The Declaration of Independence states, "*We hold these truths to be self-evident, that all men are created equal, that they are endowed by their Creator with certain unalienable Rights, that among these are Life, Liberty and the pursuit of Happiness.*" This simple statement, just a small part of the Declaration, is the backbone of the United States. Americans have died protecting this belief. The Declaration of Independence is truly the foundation for America.

A statue at Lexington, Massachusetts honors the Minutemen who stood their ground against the British in April of 1775.

GLOSSARY

colonists (KOLL-uh-nists)
America's colonists were people who lived in the original 13 colonies, before the United States became a nation. The American colonies were ruled by the King of England.

Continental Army (KON-tin-EN-tull AR-mee)
America's army, which fought the British in the War of Independence, was called the Continental Army.

Continental Congress (KON-tin-EN-tull KONG-gress)
The Continental Congress was a government made up of leaders from all 13 of America's colonies. The Continental Congress ordered and approved the writing of the Declaration of Independence.

declaration (DECK-luh-RAY-shun)
A declaration is a public announcement of something important. The Declaration of Independence announced America's freedom from British rule.

draft (DRAFT)
A draft is a rough, unfinished version of a piece of writing. Thomas Jefferson wrote the first draft of the Declaration of Independence.

independent (in-dee-PEN-dent)
An independent country is one that is not controlled by any other nation. The Declaration of Independence announced that America was an independent nation.

pamphlets (PAM-flets)
Pamphlets are small booklets. In the 1700s, pamphlets were inexpensive to print and a popular way to pass on ideas and information.

patriots (PAY-tree-uts)
The soldiers who fought for America's freedom were called Patriots.

INDEX